The Chaldean Account of the Deluge

By

George Smith

First published in 1873

Published by Left of Brain Books

Copyright © 2023 Left of Brain Books

ISBN 978-1-397-66898-1

First Edition

All rights reserved. No part of this publication may be reproduced, distributed, or transmitted in any form or by any means, including photocopying, recording, or other electronic or mechanical methods, without the prior written permission of the publisher, except in the case of brief quotations permitted by copyright law. Left of Brain Books is a division of Left Of Brain Onboarding Pty Ltd.

PUBLISHER'S PREFACE

About the Book

"This paper, which was read before the Society of Biblical Archaeology in London on Decmber 3rd, 1872, caused a sensation. George Smith (1840-76), an engraver by trade, was self-educated in Biblical and Near Eastern archeaology, mostly by studying the exhibits at the British Museum. He joined the museum as a 'repairer', piecing together fragments of tablets from Ninevah, a job which he excelled at. In 1886 he was appointed Assistant, and in 1871 he published The Phonetic Values of the Cuneiform Characters, a key reference work for reading Assyrian.

Smith started to find bits and pieces which suggested an account of a flood. In 1872, Smith found a large fragment covered with a thick deposit which, when removed, revealed a large part of the flood narrative. Reportedly, he exclaimed, "I am the first man to read that after more than two thousand years of oblivion," put the tablet on a table, and ran around the room manaically, taking off his clothes!

The tablet had the story of a deluge, which resembled the account in Genesis, but which was obviously older than the Bible. Today, we know this as the eleventh tablet of the Gilgamesh epic. As a result of this discovery, Smith got funding to go into the field in 1873, funded by a London newspaper, the Daily Telegraph. Smith uncovered more tablets with fragments of the Deluge story. In 1874 and 1876 he returned to the Middle East, under the Aegis of the British Museum. He tragically died at the age of 36 of dysentery in Aleppo, Syria, on August 19, 1876."

(Quote from sacred-texts.com)

About the Author

George Smith (1840 - 1876)

"Smith, George, Assyriologist, born at London; trained as a bank-note engraver, but attracted the attention of Sir Henry Rawlinson by his interest in cuneiform inscriptions, and in 1867 received an appointment in the British Museum; acquired great skill as an interpreter of Assyrian inscriptions, published "Annals of Assurbanipal," and in 1872 discovered a tablet with the "Chaldean Account of the Deluge"; carried through important expeditions (1871-3-6) in search of antiquities in Nineveh and other parts of Assyria, accounts of which he published; wrote also histories of Babylonia, Assyria, Sennacherib. (1840-1876)."

(Quote from fromoldbooks.org)

CONTENTS

PUBLISHER'S PREFACE
    THE CHALDEAN ACCOUNT OF THE DELUGE 1

THE CHALDEAN ACCOUNT OF THE DELUGE

by George Smith

Transactions of the Society of Biblical Archaeology 2 [1873] 213-34.

A short time back I discovered among the Assyrian tablets in the British Museum, an account of the flood; which, under the advice of our President, I now bring before the Society.

For convenience of working, I had divided the collection of Assyrian tablets in the British Museum into sections, according to the subject matter of the inscriptions.

I have recently been examining the division comprising the Mythological and Mythical tablets, and from this section I obtained a number of tablets, giving a curious series of legends and including a copy of the story of the Flood. On discovering these documents, which were much mutilated, I searched over all the collections of fragments of inscriptions, consisting of several thousands of smaller pieces, and ultimately recovered 80 fragments of these legends; by the aid of which I was enabled to restore nearly all the text of the description of the Flood, and considerable portions of the other legends. These tablets were originally at least twelve in number, forming one story or set of legends, the account of the Flood being on the eleventh tablet.

Of the inscription describing the Flood, there are fragments of three copies containing the same texts; these copies belong to the time of Assurbanipal, or about 660 years before the Christian era, and they were found in the library of that monarch in the palace at Nineveh. The original text, according to the statements on the tablets, must have belonged to the city of Erech, and it appears to have been either written in, or translated into the Semitic Babylonian, at a very early period. The date when this document was first written or translated is at present very difficult to decide, but the following are some of the evidences of its antiquity:

1st. The three Assyrian copies present a number of variant readings, which had crept into the text since the original documents were written.

2nd. The forms of the characters in the original documents were of an ancient type, and the Assyrian copyist did not always know their modern representatives, so he has left some of them in their original hieratic form.

3rd. There are a number of sentences which were originally glosses explanatory of the subjects; before the Assyrian copies were made these glosses had been already incorporated in the text and their original use lost.

It must here be noted that the Assyrian scribe has recorded for us the divisions of the lines on the original documents.

On examining the composition of the text, some marked peculiarities are apparent, which likewise show its high antiquity. one of these is the constant use of the personal pronoun nominative. In later times this was usually indicated by the verbal form, but not expressed. On comparing the Deluge text with dated texts from the time of Sargon I, it appears to be older than these, and its original composition cannot be placed later than the seventeenth century before the Christian era; while it may be much older. The text itself professes to belong to the time of a monarch whose name, written in monograms, I am unable to read phonetically; I therefore provisionally call him by the ordinary values of the signs of his name, Izdubar.

Izdubar, from the description of his reign, evidently belonged to the Mythical period; the legends given in these tablets, the offer of marriage made to him by the goddess Ishtar, the monsters living at the time, Izdubar's vision of the gods, his journey to the translated Sisit, with a curious account of a mythical conquest of Erech when the gods and spirits inhabiting that city changed themselves into animals to escape the fury of the conqueror: all these things and many others show the unhistorical nature of the epoch. From the heading of the tablets giving his history, I suppose that Izdubar lived in the epoch immediately following the Flood, and I think, likewise, that he may have been the founder of the Babylonian monarchy, perhaps the Nimrod of Scripture. This, however, is pure conjecture; so many fabulous stories were current in Babylonia respecting Izdubar that his existence may even be doubted. The fragments of the history of Izdubar, so far as I have at present examined them, remind me of the exploits and labors of Hercules, and, on the supposition that our present version of Berosus is correct as to dates, Izdubar may have been placed about 30,000 years before the Christian era. No document can belong to so remote an age. The legends of Izdubar and the account of the Flood must however belong to a very early period, for there are references to the story in the bilingual lists which were composed in Babylonia during the early Chaldean empires.

The question might here be asked, "How is it that we find an early Chaldean document from Erech transported to Nineveh, copied, and placed in the royal library there?" On this point we can show that it was a common custom for the Assyrians to obtain and copy Babylonian works, and a considerable portion of Assyrian literature consists of these copies of older standard writings.

Assurbanipal, the Assyrian monarch in whose reign the Deluge Tablets were copied, had intimate relations with the city of Erech. Erech remained faithful to him when the rest of Babylonia revolted, and to this city Assurbarripal restored the famous image of the goddess Nana, which had been carried away by the Elamites one thousand six hundred and thirty-five years before.

In order properly to understand the reason why the narrative of the Flood is introduced into the story, it will be necessary to give a short account of the tablets which precede it before giving the translation of the Deluge inscription itself.

It appears that Izdubar, the hero of these legends, flourished as before stated, in the mythical period soon after the Flood, and the center of most of his exploits was the city of Erech, now called Warka, which must have been one of the most ancient cities in the world. Four cities only are mentioned in these inscriptions, Babel, Erech, Surippak, and Nipur. Two of these, Babel and Erech, are the first two capitals of Nimrod, and the last one, Nipur, according to the Talmud, is the same as Calneh the fourth city of Nimrod. Of the first five tablets of the history of Izdubar I have not recognized any fragments, but in the mass of material which I have collected it is possible that some portions may be long to this part of the story.

The following passage forms the opening of the sixth tablet and shows the style of the writing. Before giving the translation I must notice that in various places the tablets are broken and the texts defective: as I cannot point out each of these defective passages, I will endeavor to indicate them by pausing in my reading.

1. . . . . . Belesu, he despised Belesu
2. like a bull his country he ascended after him
3. he destroyed him, and his memorial perished
4. the country was subdued, and after he took the crown
5. Izdubar put on his crown, and after he took the crown
6. for the favor of Izdubar, the princess Ishtar lifted her eyes.
7. And she spake thus, "Izdubar thou shalt be husband
8. thy word me shall bind in bonds,
9. thou shalt be husband and I will be thy wife,
10. thou shalt drive in a chariot of Ukni stone and gold,
11. of which its body is gold and splendid its pole
12. thou shalt ride in days of great glory
13. to Bitani, in which is the country where the pine trees grow.
14. Bitani at thy entrance
15. to the Euphrates shall kiss thy feet.
16. There shall be in subjection under thee, kings, lords, and princes.
17. The tribute of the mountains and plains they shall bring to thee, taxes
18. . . . . they shall give thee, thy herds and flocks shall bring forth twins
19. . . . . the mule shall be swift
20. . . . . in the chariot shall be strong and not weak
21. . . . . in the yoke. A rival shall not be permitted."

Ishtar, who was the same as Venus, was queen of beauty, but some what inconstant, for she had already a husband, a deity, called the "Son of Life"; she however led her husband a poor life, and of this Izdubar reminds her in his answer to her offer.

One of the next exploits of Izdubar and Heabani his servant was the conquest of the winged bull, a monster supposed to have existed in those days; but I must pass over this and other matters, to approach the subject of the Flood.

In course of time Izdubar, the conqueror of kings and monsters, the ruler of peoples, fell into some illness and came to fear death, man's last great enemy. Now, the Babylonians believed in the existence of a patriarch named Sisit, the Xisuthrus of the Greeks, who was supposed to have been translated and to have attained to immortality without death. Izdubar, according to the notions of the time, resolved to seek Sisit, to ascertain how he became immortal, that he might attain to a similar honor. The passage reads as follows:

1. Izdubar to Heabani his servant
2. bitterly lamented and lay down on the ground
3. I the account took from Heabani and
4. weakness entered into my soul
5. death I feared and I lay down on the ground
6. to find Sisit son of Ubaratutu
7. the road I was taking and joyfully I went
8. to the shadows of the mountains I took at night
9. the gods I saw and I feared
10. . . . . . . to Sin I prayed
11. and before the gods my supplication came
12. peace they gave unto me
13. and they sent unto me it dream.

The dream of Izdubar is unfortunately very mutilated, few fragments of it remaining, and his subsequent journey is not in much better condition. It appears that he went through a number of adventures, and three men are represented, in one place, to be telling each other the story of these adventures.

After long wanderings, Izdubar falls into company with a seaman named Urbamsi, a name similar to the Orchamus of the Greeks. Izdubar and Urhamsi fit out a vessel to continue the search for Sisit, and they sail along for a month and fifteen days, and arrive at some region near the mouth of the Euphrates, where Sisit was supposed to dwell. in this journey by water there are fresh adventures and, in their course, Urharnsi tells Izdubar of the waters of death, of which he states, "The waters of death thy hands will not cleanse."

At the time when Izdubar and Urhamsi are approaching him, Sisit is sleeping.The tablet here is too mutilated to inform us how they came to see each other, but it appears probable from the context that Sisit was seen in company with his wife, a long distance off, separated from Izdubar by a stream.

Unable to cross this water which divided the mortal from the immortal, Izdubar appears to have called to Sisit and asked his momentous question on life and death. The question asked by Izdubar and the first part of the answer of Sisit are lost by the mutilation of the tablet. The latter part of the speech of Sisit, which is preserved, relates to the danger of death, its universality, &c. It winds up as follows: "The goddess Mamitu the maker of fate to them their fate has appointed, she has fixed death and life, but of death the day is not known." These words, which close the first speech of Sisit, bring us to the end of the tenth tablet; the next one, the eleventh, is the most important of the series, as it contains the history of the Flood.

The eleventh tablet opens with a speech of Izdubar, who now asks Sisit how he became immortal, and Sisit, fit answering, relates the story of the Flood and his own piety as the reason why he was translated. The following is the translation of this tablet:

1. Izdubar after this manner said to Sisit afar off,
2. ". . . . . . Sisit
3. The account do thou tell to me,
4. The account do thou tell to me,
5. . . . . . to the midst to make war
6. . . . . . I come up after thee.
7. say how thou hast done it, and in the circle of the gods life thou hast gained."
8. Sisit after this manner said to Izdubar,
9. "I will reveal to thee, Izdubar, the concealed story,
10. and the wisdom of the gods I will relate to thee.
11. The city Surippak the city which thou hast established . . . . placed
12. was ancient, and the gods within it
13. dwelt, a tempest . . . . . their god, the great gods
14. . . . . Anu
15. . . . . Bel
16. . . . . Ninip
17. . . . . lord of Hades
18. their will revealed in the midst of . . . . .
19 . . . . hearing and he spoke to me thus
20. Surippakite son of Ubaratutu
21. make a great ship for thee . . . .
22. I will destroy the sinners and life . . . . .
23. cause to go in the seed of life all of it, to preserve them
24. the ship which thou shalt make
25. . . . cubits shall be the measure of its length, and
26. . . . cubits the amount of its breadth and its height.
27. Into the deep launch it."
28. I perceived and said to Hea my lord,
29. "Hea my lord this that thou commandest me
30. I will perform, it shall be done.
31. . . . . army and host

32. Hea opened his mouth and spake, and said to me his servant,
33. . . . . thou shalt say unto them,
34. . . . . he has turned from me and
35. . . . . .fixed . . . .

Here there are about fifteen lines entirely lost. The absent passage probably described part of the building of the ark.

51. it . . . .
52. which in . . . .
53. strong . . . . . . I brought
54. on the fifth day . . . . . it
55. in its circuit 14 measures . . . . its sides
56. 14 measures it measured . . . . over it
57. I Placed its roof on it . . . . . I enclosed it
58. I rode in it, for the sixth time I . . . . . . for the seventh time
59. into the restless deep . . . . . for the . . . . time
60. its planks the waters within it admitted,
61. I saw breaks and holes . . . . . . my hand placed
62. three measures of bitumen I poured over the outside,
63. three measures of bitumen I poured over the inside
64. three measures the men carrying its baskets took they . . . . . fixed an altar
65. I unclosed the altar . . . . . the altar for an offering
66. two measures the altar . . . . Pazziru the pilot
67. for . . . . slaughtered oxen
68. of . . . . in that day also
69. . . . . altar and grapes
70. . . . . like the waters of a river and
71. . . . . like the day I covered and
72. . . . . when . . . . . covering my hand placed,
73. . . . .and Shamas . . . . the material of the ship completed,
74. . . . . strong and

75. reeds I spread above and below.
76. . . . . went in two thirds of it.
77. All I possessed I collected it, all I possessed I collected of silver,
78. all I possessed I collected of gold,
79. all I possessed I collected of the seed of life, the whole
80. I caused to go up into the ship, all my male and female servants,
81. the beasts of the field, the animals of the field, and the sons of the army all of them, I caused to go up.
82. A flood Shamas made, and
83. he spake saying in the night, 'I will cause it to rain from heaven heavily;
84. enter to the midst of the ship, and shut thy door,'
85. A flood he raised, and
86. he spake saying in the night, 'I will cause it to rain from heaven heavily.'
87. In the day that I celebrated his festival
88. the day which he had appointed; fear I had,
89. I entered to the midst of the ship, and shut my door;
90. to guide the ship, to Buzursadirabi the pilot,
91. the palace I gave to his hand.
92. The raging of a storm in the morning
93. arose, from the horizon of heaven extending and wide
94. Vul in the midst of it thundered, and
95. Nebo and Saru went in front;
96. the throne bearers went over mountains and plains;
97. the destroyer Nergal overturned;
98. Ninip went in front, and cast down;
99. the spirits carried destruction;
100. in their glory they swept the earth;
101. of Vul the flood, reached to heaven;
102. the bright earth to a waste was turned;
103. the surface of the earth, like . . . . it swept;
104. it destroyed all life, from the face of the earth . . . . .

105. the strong tempest over the people, reached to heaven.
106. Brother saw not his brother, it did not spare the people. In heaven
107. the gods feared the tempest, and
108. Sought refuge; they ascended to the heaven of Anu.
109. The gods, like dogs with tails hidden, couched down.
110. Spake Ishtar a discourse,
111. uttered the great goddess her speech
112. 'The world to sin has turned, and
113. then I in the presence of the gods prophesied evil;
114. when I prophesied in the presence of the gods evil,
115. to evil were devoted all my people, and I prophesied
116. thus, 'I have begotten man and let him not
117. like the sons of the fishes fill the sea.'
118. The gods concerning the spirits, were weeping with her:
119. the gods in seats, seated in lamentation;
120. covered were their lips for the coming evil.
121. Six days and nights
122. passed, the wind tempest and storm overwhelmed,
123. on the seventh day in its course, was calmed the storm, and all the tempest
124. which had destroyed like an earthquake,
125. quieted. The sea he caused to dry, and the wind and tempest ended.
126. I was carried through the sea. The doer of evil,
127. and the whole of mankind who turned to sin,
128. like reeds their corpses floated.
129. I opened the window and the light broke in, over my refuge
130. it passed, I sat still and
131. over my refuge came peace.
132. I was carried over the shore, at the boundary of the sea.
133. For twelve measures it ascended over the land.
134. To the country of Nizir, went the ship;

135. the mountain of Nizir stopped the ship, and to pass over it, it was not able.
136. The first day and the second day, the mountain of Nizir the same.
137. The third day and the fourth day, the mountain of Nizir the same.
138. The fifth and sixth, the mountain of Nizir the same.
139. On the seventh day in the course of it
140. I sent forth a dove, and it left. The dove went and searched and
141. a resting place it did not find, and it returned.
142. I sent forth a swallow, and it left. The swallow went and searched and
143. a resting place it did not find, and it returned.
144. I sent forth a raven, and it left.
145. The raven went, and the corpses on the waters it saw, and
146. it did eat, it swam, and wandered away, and did not return.
147. I sent the animals forth to the four winds I poured out a libation
148. I built an altar on the peak of the mountain,
149. by sevens herbs I cut,
150. at the bottom of them, I placed reeds, pines, and simgar.
151. The gods collected at its burning, the gods collected at its good burning.
152. the gods like flies over the sacrifice gathered,
153. From of old also, the great God in his course,
154. the great brightness of Arm had created; when the glory
155. of these gods, as of Ukni stone, on my countenance I could not endure;
156. in those days I prayed that for ever I might not endure.
157. May the gods come to my altar;
158. may Bel not come to my altar
159. for he did not consider and had made a tempest
160. and my people he had consigned to the deep
161. from of old, also Bel in his course

162. saw the ship, and went Bel with anger filled to the gods and spirits;
163. let not any one come out alive, let not a man be saved from the deep.
164. Ninip his mouth opened and spake, and said to the warrior Bel,
165. 'who then will be saved,' Hea the words understood,
166. and Hea knew all things,
167. Hea his mouth opened and spake, and said to the warrior Bel,
168. 'Thou prince of the gods, warrior,
169. when thou art angry a tempest thou makest,
170. the doer of sin did his sin, the doer of evil did his evil,
171. may the exalted not be broken, may the captive not be delivered;
172. instead of thee making a tempest, may lions increase and men be reduced;
173. instead of thee making a tempest, may leopards increase, and men be reduced;
174. instead of thee making a tempest, may a famine happen, and the country be destroyed;
175. instead of thee making a tempest, may pestilence increase, and men be destroyed.'
176. I did not peer into the wisdom of the gods,
177. reverent and attentive a dream they sent, and the wisdom of the gods he heard.
178. When his judgment was accomplished, Bel went up to the midst of the ship,
179. he took my hand and brought me out, me
180. he brought out, he caused to bring my wife to my side,
181. he purified the country, he established in a covenant and took the people
182. in the presence of Sisit and the people.

183. When Sisit and his wife and the people to be like the gods were carried away,
184. then dwelt Sisit in a remote place at the mouth of the rivers.
185. They took me and in a remote place at the mouth of the rivers they seated me.
186. When to thee whom the gods have chosen thee, and
187. the life which thou has sought after, thou shalt gain
188. this do, for six days and seven nights
189. like I say also, in bonds bind him
190. the way like a storm shall be laid upon him."
191. Sisit after this manner, said to his wife
192. "I announce that the chief who grasps at life
193. the way like a storm shall be laid upon him."
194. His wife after this manner, said to Sisit afar off,
195. "Purify him and let the man be sent away,
196. the road that lie came, may he return in peace,
197. the great gate open, and may he return to his country."
198. Sisit after this manner, said to his wife,
199. "The cry of a man alarms thee,
200. this do, his scarlet cloth place on his head."
201. And the day when he ascended the side of the ship
202. she did, his scarlet cloth she placed on his head,
203. and the day when he ascended on the side of the ship,

The next four lines describe seven things done to Izdubar before he was purified. The passage is obscure and does not concern the Flood, so I have not translated it.

208. Izdubar after this manner, said to Sisit afar off,
209. "This way, she has done, I come up
210. joyfully, my strength thou givest me."
211. Sisit after this manner said to Izdubar
212. . . . . thy scarlet cloth
213. . . . . I have lodged thee

214. . . . .

The five following lines, which are mutilated, refer again to the seven matters for purifying Izdubar; this passage, like the former one, I do not translate.

219. Izdubar after this manner said to Sisit afar off
220. . . . . Sisit to thee may we not come.

From here the text is much mutilated, and it will be better to give a general account of its contents than to attempt a strict translation, especially as this part is not so interesting as the former part of the tablet.

Lines 221 and 223 mention some one who was taken and dwelt with Death. Lines 224 to 235 gives a speech of Sisit to the seaman Urhamsi, directing him how to cure Izdubar, who, from the broken passages, appears to have been suffering from some form of skin disease. Izdubar was to be dipped in the sea, when beauty was to spread over his skin once more. In lines 236 to 241 the carrying out of these directions and the cure of Izdubar are recorded.

The tablet then reads as follows:

242. Izdubar and Urhamsi rode in the boat
243. where they placed them they rode
244. His wife after this manner said to Sisit afar off,
245. "Izdubar goes away, he is satisfied, he performs
246. that which thou hast given him and returns to his country."
247. And he heard, and after Izdubar
248. he went to the shore
249. Sisit after this manner said to Izdubar,

250. "Izdubar thou goest away thou art satisfied, thou performest
251. That which I have given thee and thou returnest to thy country
252. I have revealed to thee Izdubar the concealed story."

Lines 253 to 262, which are very mutilated, give the conclusion of the speech of Sisit, and then state that after hearing it, Izdubar took great stones and piled them up as a memorial of these events.

Lines 263 to 289 give in a very mutilated condition subsequent speeches and doings of Izdubar and Urhanisi. In this part journeys are mentioned of 10 and 20 kaspu, or 70 and 140 miles; a lion is also spoken of, but there is no further allusion to the Flood. These lines close the inscription, and are followed by a colophon which gives the heading of the next tablet, and the statement that this (the Flood Tablet) is the 11th tablet in the series giving the history of Izdubar, and that it is a copy of the ancient inscription.

Before entering into the details of the tablet, I must first refer to the accounts of the Deluge given in the Bible, and by Berosus, the Chaldean historian, as I shall have to compare these with the Cuneiform record.

The Biblical account of the Deluge, contained in the sixth to the ninth chapters of Genesis, is of course familiar to us all, so I will only give the outline of the narrative.

According to the Book of Genesis, as man mutiplied on the earth, the whole race turned to evil, except the family of Noah. On account of the wickedness of man, the Lord determined to destroy the world by a flood, and gave command to Noah to build an ark, 300 cubits long, 50 cubits broad, and 30 cubits high. Into this ark Noah entered according to the command of the Lord, taking with him his family, and pairs of each animal. After seven days the Flood commenced in the 600th year of Noah, the seventeenth day of the second month, and after 150 days the ark rested upon the mountains of Ararat, on the seventeenth day of the seventh month. We are then told that after 40 days Noah opened the window of the ark and sent forth a raven which did not return. He then sent forth a dove, which finding no rest for the sole of her foot, returned to him. Seven days after he sent forth the dove a second time, she returned to him with an olive leaf in her mouth. Again, after seven days, he sent forth the dove which returned to him no more. The Flood was dried up in the 601st year, on the first day of the first month, and on the twenty-seventh day of the second month, Noah removed from the ark and afterwards built an altar and offered sacrifices.

The Chaldean account of the Flood, as given by Berosus, I have taken from Cory's Ancient Fragments, pages 26 to 29, as follows:

"After the death of Ardates, his son Xisuthrus reigned eighteen sari. In his time happened a great Deluge, the history of which is thus described: The Deity, Cronos, appeared to him in a vision, and warned him that upon the fifteenth day of the month Daesius, there would be a flood, by which mankind would be destroyed. He, therefore, enjoined him to write a history of the beginning, procedure, and conclusion of all things; and to bury it in the City of the Sun at Sippara; and to build a vessel, and take with him into it his friends and relations; and to convey on board everything necessary to sustain life, together with all the different animals, both birds and quadrupeds, and trust himself fearlessly to the deep. Having asked the Deity whither he was to sail? he was answered, 'To the Gods'; upon which he offered up a prayer for the good of mankind. He then obeyed the Divine admonition, and built a vessel five stadia in length, and two in breadth. Into this he put every thing which he had prepared: and last of all conveyed into it his wife, his children, and his friends.

"After the Flood had been upon the earth, and was in time abated, Xisuthrus sent out birds from the vessel, which not finding any food, nor any place whereupon they might rest their feet, returned to him again. After an interval of some days he sent them forth a second time, and they now returned with their feet tinged with mud. He made a trial a third time with these birds, but they returned to him no more: from whence he judged that the surface of the earth had appeared above the waters. He, therefore, made an opening in the vessel, and upon looking out found that it was stranded upon the side of some mountain, upon which he immediately quitted it with his wife, his daughter, and the pilot. Xisuthrus then paid his adoration to the earth, and having constructed an altar, offered sacrifices to the gods, and, with those who had come out of the vessel with him, disappeared. "They, who remained within, finding that their companions did not return, quitted the vessel with many lamentations, and called con tinually on the name of Xisuthrus. Him they saw no more; but they could distinguish his voice in the air, and could hear him admonish them to pay due regard to religion; and likewise informed them that it was upon account of his piety that he was translated to live with the gods, that his wife, and daughter, and the pilot, had obtained the same honor. To this he added that they should return to Babylonia, and as it was ordained, search for the writings at Sippara, which they were to make known to all mankind; moreover, that the place wherein they were was the land of Armenia.

"The rest having heard these words, offered sacrifices to the gods, and taking a circuit, journeyed towards Babylonia.

"The vessel being thus stranded in Armenia, some part of it yet remains in the Corcyraean mountains."

In pages 33 and 34 of Cory's Fragments there is a second version, as follows:

"And then Sisithrus. To him the deity of Cronos foretold that on the fifteenth day of the month Daesius there would be a deluge of rain: and he commanded him to deposit all the writings whatever which were in his possession, in the City of the Sun at Sippara. Sisithrus, when he had complied with these commands, sailed immediately to Armenia, and was presently inspired by God. Upon the third day after the cessation of the rain Sisithrus sent out birds, by way of experiment, that he might judge whether the Flood had subsided. But the birds passing over an unbounded sea, without finding any place of rest, re turned again to Sisithrus. This he repeated with other birds. And when upon the third trial he succeeded, for the birds then returned with their feet stained with mud, the gods translated him from among men. With respect to the vessel, which yet remains in Armenia, it is a custom of the inhabitants to form bracelets and amulets of its wood."

There are several other accounts of the Flood in the traditions of different ancient nations; these, however, are neither so full nor so precise as the account of Berosus, and their details so far as they are given differ more from the Biblical narrative, so I shall not notice them now, but pass at once to the examination of the text.

In comparing the text of the Deluge Tablet with the accounts in the Bible and Berosus, the first point that meets us is the consideration of the proper names. This is the least satisfactory part of the subject, for, while the Greek forms show variant readings and have evidently been corrupted, the Cuneiform names on the other hand, being written mostly in monograms, are difficult to render phonetically. The father of the hero of the Flood bears in the inscriptions the name Ubara-tutu which ought to correspond to one of the Greek forms, Otiártes or Ardátes; the resemblance however cannot be called a close one. The hero of the Flood I have provisionally called Sisit; he corresponds, of course, to the Greek Xisuthrus, but no comparison of the two names can be made until we know the phonetic reading of the Cuneiform name. Neither the Cuneiform nor the Greek names appear to have any connection with the Biblical Lamech and Noah. In the opening of the account of the Flood there is a noticeable difference between the Cuneiform and Biblical narratives, for while in the Jewish account one God only is men tioned, the Cuneiform inscription mentions all the principal gods of the early Babylonian Pantheon as engaged in bringing about the Flood.

The Cuneiform account agrees with the Biblical narrative in making the Deluge a divine punishment for the wickedness of the world; this point is omitted in the Greek accounts of Berosus.

The gods having resolved on the Deluge, the deity whom we have hitherto provisionally called Hea announces the coming event to Sisit. Now, in the account of Berosus, the god who announces the Deluge is stated to be Cronos; so this passage gives us the Cuneiform name of the deity identified by the Greeks with Cronos. The Greek account states that the communication of the coming Deluge was made in a dream. From the context it is probable that the Cuneiform account stated the same, but the text is here mutilated so that the point cannot be decided.

The dimensions of the vessel in the inscription are unfortunately lost by a fracture which has broken off both numbers; the passage, which is otherwise complete, shows that the dimensions were expressed in cubits as in the Biblical account, but while Genesis makes the ark 50 cubits broad and 30 cubits high, the inscription states that the height and breadth were the same.

The greater part of the description of the building of the ark is lost. In the latter part of the account which is preserved, there is mention of the trial of the vessel by launching it into the sea, when defects being found which admitted the water, the outside and inside were coated with bitumen. These details have no parallel either in the Bible or Berosus. The description of the filling of the ark agrees in general with the two other accounts, but it differs from Genesis in not mentioning the sevens of clean animals and in including others beside the family of the builder.

The month and day when the Deluge commenced, which are given in the Bible and Berosus, are not mentioned in the text, unless the fifth day, mentioned in a mutilated passage, is part of this date.

The description of the Flood in this inscription is very vivid; it is said to have been so terrible that the gods, fearing it, ascended to the heaven of Arm, that it is the highest and furthest heaven, the destruction of the human race is recorded, and the corpses of the wicked are said to have floated on the surface of the Flood.

With regard to the duration of the Deluge, there appears to be a serious difference between the Bible and the inscription. According to the account in the Book of Genesis, the Flood commenced on the seventeenth day of the second month, the ark rested on Ararat after one hundred and fifty days on the seventeenth day of the seventh month, and the complete drying up of the Flood was not until the twenty seventh day of the second month in the following year. The inscription, on the other hand, states that the Flood abated on the seventh day, and that the ship remained seven days on the mountain before the sending out of the birds.

On this point it must be remarked that some Biblical critics consider that there are two versions of the Flood story in Genesis itself, and that these two differ as to the duration of the Flood.

The Greek account of Berosus is silent as to the duration of the Deluge.

With regard to the mountain on which the ark rested there is a difference between the Bible and the inscription, which is more apparent than real. The Book of Genesis states that the ark rested on the mountains of Ararat. According to the popular notion this refers to the mountain of Ararat, in Armenia; but these mountains may have been anywhere within the ancient territory of Ararat, and some Commentators looking at the passage in Berosus, where the ark is stated to have rested in the Gordiaean mountains, have inclined to place the mountain referred to in the Kurdish mountains, east of Assyria. In accordance with this indication the inscription states that the ship rested on the mountain of Nizir.

Now, the position of Nizir can be determined from the inscription of Assur-nazir-pal, king of Assyria. He made an expedition to this region, and starting from an Assyrian city, near Arbela, crossed the Lower Zab, and marching eastward between latitudes 35 and 36, arrived at the mountains of Nizir.

These mountains of Nizir thus lay east of Assyria, but they form part of a series of mountain chains extending to the north-west into Armenia.

The vessel being stranded on the mountain, the Bible, Berosus, and the inscription all agree that trial was made by birds in order to ascertain if the Flood had subsided; but in the details of these trials there are curious differences in all three narratives. According to the Book of Genesis, a raven was sent out first, which did not return; a dove was sent next, which finding no resting place returned to Noah. Seven days later the dove was sent out again, and returned with an olive leaf; and seven days after, on the dove being sent out again, it returned no more.

The account of Berosus mentions the sending out of the birds, but does not mention what kinds were tried. On the first trial the birds are said to have returned, and on the second trial likewise, this time with mud on their feet. On the third occasion they did not return.

The inscription states that, first, a dove was sent out, which finding no resting place returned. On the second occasion a swallow was sent, which also returned. The third time a raven was sent out, which feeding on the corpses floating on the water, wandered away and did not return. Thus, the inscription agrees with the Bible as to the sending out of the raven and dove, but adds to these the trial of the swallow, which is not in Genesis. In the number of the trials it agrees with Berosus, who has three, while Genesis has four. On the other hand there is no mention of the dove returning with an olive leaf, as in Genesis, and of the birds having their feet stained with Mud, as in Berosus.

In the statement of the building of the altar, and offering sacrifice after leaving the ark, all three accounts agree; but in the subsequent matter there is an important difference between the Bible and the inscription, for while the Bible represents Noah as living for many years after the Flood, the inscription on the other hand agrees with Berosus in making Sisit to be translated like the gods. This translation is in the Bible recorded of Enoch, the ancestor of Noah.

On reviewing the evidence it is apparent that the events of the Flood narrated in the Bible and the inscription are the same, and occur in the same order; but the minor differences in the details show that the inscription embodies a distinct and independent tradition.

In spite of a striking similarity in style, which shows itself in several places, the two narratives belong to totally distinct peoples. The Biblical account is the version of an inland people, the name of the ark in Gene sis means a chest or box, and not a ship; there is no notice of the sea, or of launching, no pilots are spoken of, no navigation is mentioned. The inscription on the other hand belongs to a maritime people, the ark is called a ship, the ship is launched into the sea, trial is made of it, and it is given in charge of a pilot.

The Cuneiform inscription, after giving the history of the Flood down to the sacrifice of Sisit, when he came out of the ark, goes back to the former part of the story, and mentions the god Bel in particular as the maker of the tempest or deluge; there appears to be a slight inconsistency between this and the former part of the inscription which suggests the question whether the Chaldean narrative itself may not have been compiled from two distinct and older accounts.

It is remarkable that the oldest traditions of the early Babylonians seem to center round the Persian Gulf. From this sea, Oannes the fish god is supposed to have arisen, and the composite monsters who followed him in the antediluvian period came from the same region. Into this sea the ark was launched, and after the subsiding of the Deluge when Sisit was translated, he dwelt in this neighborhood. To this sea also came the great hero Izdubar, and was cured, and here he heard the story of the Flood.

In conclusion I would remark that this account of the Deluge opens to us a new field of inquiry in the early part of the Bible history. The question has often been asked, "What is the origin of the accounts of the antediluvians, with their long lives so many times greater than the longest span of human life? Where was Paradise, the abode of the first parents of mankind? From whence comes the story of the flood, the ark, of the birds?" Various conflicting answers have been given to these important questions, while evidence on these subjects before the Greek period has been entirely wanting. The Cuneiform inscriptions are now shedding a new light on these questions, and supplying material which future scholars will have to work out. Following this inscription, we may expect many other discoveries throwing light on these ancient periods, until we are able to form a decisive opinion on the many great questions involved. It would be a mistake to suppose that with the translation and commentary on an inscription like this the matter is ended. The origin, age, and history of the legend have to be traced, and it has to be compared with the many similar stories current among various nations.

All these accounts, together with considerable portions of the ancient mythologies have, I believe, a common origin in the Plains of Chaldea. This country the cradle of civilization, the birthplace of the arts and sciences, for 2,000 years has been in ruins; its literature, containing the most precious records of antiquity, is scarcely known to us, except from the texts the Assyrians copied, but beneath its mounds and ruined cities, now awaiting exploration, lay, together with older copies of this Deluge text, other legends and histories of the earliest civilization in the world.

www.ingramcontent.com/pod-product-compliance
Lightning Source LLC
Chambersburg PA
CBHW051607010526
44119CB00056B/812